The Art of Living

Jeanine Williams

BookLeaf Publishing

India | USA | UK

Presentation by *BookLeaf Publishing*

Web: www.bookleafpub.com

E-mail: info@bookleafpub.com

ISBN: 978-93-5761-230-2

First edition 2022

DEDICATION

I dedicate my poetry to the children sitting high on hay bales and dreams, in the height of summer, with their arms to the sky feeling like they're on top of the world. May you know them, hold them, and be them.

ACKNOWLEDGEMENT

I would like to thank those who have served as inspiration for my writings and also those who supported me in my journey back to art. My Mother and Father, Natalie, Julian, Lucas, Phil, Elaine, Kate, Jacqueline, as well as my family in Nova Scotia, Moe, Euan, Jordanne, Ryan and the congregation of Friends Church.

PREFACE

I was inspired to write this book in the throes and woes of the global pandemic COVID-19. The tumultuous period of time gifted us all with the opportunity to slow down and sit with introspection. My time in reflection lead me to a quieter life that I keep exciting with Art. I decided, given my Jill-of-all-Trades persona, to illustrate each poem as an art form. From minimalistic painting to Verismo Opera, there's a slice of art for everybody.

Mourning Song

"I sing like a bird!"
I used to say, as if I understood,
But I do now

A bird sings at the break of day
In the creeping, quiet twilight, our voices are
silenced

No one wants to hear your song in the darkest
hour,
They are all sleeping
Let them sleep.

You'll sing your song with the dawn,
While they begin to stretch and yawn
Your voice rings out, a truth, a breath, an alarm

Kintsugi

"I just want to be a beautiful salad bowl"

She spoke in guarded metaphors
 She was practically begging, with her
thinly-veiled nihilism, to find some meaning or
purpose

Soon however, came peace in resolve
Her body expanded, and she shone as if molten
gold had, in newly soft and rounded edges,
found its home

Little Black Book

My journal is filled with your name
I see a thousand black marks, burned into the
page
There is mention of the temporary companions
and disappointing emails, though they are
eclipsed in flame

I'm not entirely sure if I am blinded by the
flickering of my lighter or the damning fire in
my heart

I hope to put it out, be it joint or organ
Now I wonder what inferno will blaze, as write
my own name instead

Cinema

If you go to the movies, do you suppose you will
be entertained?

After all, you've sat in the dark alone before, and
hoped for something more
It's a bore, watching the frames race just seated,
as vertigo breaks you in

You may feel stuck, like some outsider, as your
eyes glaze over the screen
 You're in the dark, strangers all about; It's not
your story.

Poetry

Words can hurt.

Worse, is the deafening silence of words that never came.

These are the poems you may never hear.

Mimì

Oh, do go on!
Tell me more of far off places.
Describe hovering castles high above, and the
dreams that fly you there.
I want to feel cold hands, and taste violet lips. I
want to go where no one really knows quite
where you are, but they imagine it as somewhere
beautiful.
If we venture there, I couldn't possibly wear
white, I just love an adventure!
I will wear pink, and you can call me whatever
suits you, or perhaps I should say, whatever suits
me

Dialectical Thinking

It isn't half-full, nor is it half-empty,

It's pouring down the sides or else bone-dry,
hollow

My cup runneth over, then I'm starved with thirst

I'm a tall glass of roulette and I hope you're here
to gamble

Architecture

I didn't realize the picket fence would be quite so tall.

That reverie, so close, just beyond this wall.

Chefery

Eat.

Savour sweet honey draped upon each apples
skin
Languish in flasks of flowing wine, whisky, and
gin
Stock the cupboard nightly, with all the finest
cheese
And fret not of any cost, please

Treat yourself with goodness.

"Five-star taste does have a lofty price."

"You're expensive, Mabel."

But when you peer below the lushious garden
her lashes provide, you will understand
Why good things cost so much

Spoken Word

I don't know how much will be said, until I can
say, I've said everything I want to say

These feelings boiled, while tears washed my
bed of you
I now sleep in my own trembling arms

I've written from the bottom of a bottle, trying to
drown instead in art
I paint, even dance on paper, and these canvases
become an unhung gallery, cluttering my kitchen
floor

Brevity eludes my artistry

Oh, How People Will Go!

Today is the day!
You'll leave very quickly and soon get away

Be your name Katie or Jackie or Stu
Or Julie Ann Van Hullabaloo,

Your carriage is set to arrive around 8:00
So pick up your pace, you don't want to be late

Any and all can ride this fine eve,
Though watery eyes will leak as you leave

Nat with a hat, that looks quite like a doll, with
her parents beside, so proud and so tall,
Will be driving the coach that will carry you all

Don't look behind or you'll find a sad frown, a
smile, all-mixed up, and stuck upside down,
From one lonely girl, left in this ghost town

But if you listen closely you'll hear her say
"It starts today. I'm off to great places, up, up
and away!"

Dragging About

The place where fire and water meet appears as
a train station

They do not arrive in opposition
They embrace, in a hazy billowing steam

There is a softness in the cooling peace of blue
And an electricity found in the brawn of red

Race to find that temperature that will boil your
blood, and cleanse your spirit
The flames will envelope your words
The river will rush into your hands

When you've decided, climb aboard
You can take both if time affords, and if you are
an explorer

If you're on an adventure, you should toss your
map
The best part of getting lost is finding yourself

Travelling

There's a globe on my windowsill

There's a collection of maps and a small vintage
compass shelved above my bed
There's also a bicycle statue, a museum of
stamps, and a storm glass residing on my
bookshelf

I've adorned my home with my biggest secret,
I have no idea where I'm going

The Ballet

On highest pointe your toes will raise
Though both are bruised, and battered
Now lean down to meet his gaze
Your feet and heart, both shattered

Tis not a tap, or jiving swing
This is a dance of grace
Balancé into the ring,
To tentative embrace

The twirling tulle and brushing skin
Are measured, stiff and rhythmic
Yet see his eyes possessed by sin
You drop the farce and gimmick

It's better now, you dancing free,
Than chained to one not meant to be

Heaven and Earth

The Lady in White is sitting on my right
shoulder
There's a demon in red dancing on my left
shoulder
They both whisper songs no one else can hear

The Sculptor

Her hands look strong
Perhaps she is a sculptor
I see her rushing feet and spinning mind

It's a beautiful process creating, molding and
shaping the clay
I have seen the lines around her eyes harden, as
she revels in Creation

When the glaze is set and the kiln has fired, the
sculptors job is done
And yet, her hands work harder still

DJ Healing

I'm Still Standing, and I'm feeling like a
Champion.
Come to my desert and you can watch me
SUPERBLOOM!

It took time to get here...
66 Days after I got my drivers license I took a
trip to Joshua Tree with the 1.

Breaking free from the Reverie I was Lonely,
I felt like some Mad Man.
However, I have an Elastic Heart and as I
watched my tears ricochet, I knew
"this is me trying"

I understand I had to Lose You To Love Me.
It was truly a gift to embrace myself as I
watched you Slide Away,
Because now I know, I'm my own Soulmate.

My mind has been kind since then.
"Hey Doll, it's gunna be okay."

I hold this peace firmly, in fervent prayer:
Lord, make me an instrument of thy peace

I've kept these words prepped at my lips to live
as I love, and see God in everyone.
"Call Me Mother,"
I hear call out in response

Feeling Her, and seeking God is simply
Whatever We Feel.
I know I'm not done, and I don't intend to ever
be, so watch me dance and please,
Don't Stop Me Now

The Intent of Baked Goods

Who bakes for the Baker?
Who sings sweet lullabies for the Singer?
Who holds the Mother, and strokes her soft hair?
Who will give to The Giver?

Minimalism

A blank canvas is almost more telling
Than that drenched in rainbows of passion

Potential is ever so lovely

Book Up, Nose Down

Have you got anything new?
I was here yesterday, but I flipped through the
chapters so fast
I need something new and exciting!
I want to explore, learn, and vanish
These books make me sit in my grief, revel in
pride, and forget the time

All You Need Is Love

Love Love Love Love Love Love Love Love
Love Love Love Love Love Love Love Love
Love Love Love Love Love Love Love Love
Love Love Love Love Love Love Love Love
Love Love Love Love Love Love Love Love
Love Love Love Love Love Love Love Love

I'm sorry if that doesn't read as poetry,
But if your heart is open I think you'll find that
Love is indistinguishable from Art